十二月的節日

Customs, Traditions and Landmarks | Non-Fiction Series

Copyright © 2022 by Level Learning, INC. and Washington Yu Ying PCS™
Original and Edited Text Copyright © 2022 by Washington Yu Ying PCS™

All rights reserved. No part of this book in whole or part may be reproduced without written permission from the publisher.

Published by Level Learning, INC.

Content Contributors:
Washington Yu Ying PCS™
Level Learning - Ya-Ching Chang

Illustrations by: Josh Taira

Leveling classification based on Level Learning standard. For full description, visit www.levellearning.com

ISBN 978-1-64040-025-2
Traditional Chinese Edition

About Level Learning:
Level Learning provides a literacy focused curriculum specifically designed for K-12 Chinese as a Second Language classrooms. Our program offers 20 levels of specific and detailed objectives, leveled texts and passages, mastery-based online assessment, and analytics to enable data-driven instruction. Level Learning reading curriculum for both literature and informational text emphasize grammar and comprehension skills to help teachers develop confident and independent Chinese language readers. The non-fiction series of books are specifically designed to support our informational text course based on multiple national standards. To learn more about our entire offering, visit www.levellearning.com

About Washington Yu Ying PCS™:
Washington Yu Ying PCS is a Mandarin English dual language immersion International Baccalaureate (IB) World school. Yu Ying's mission is to inspire and prepare young people to create a better world by challenging them to reach their full potential in a nurturing Chinese/English educational environment. Yu Ying's comprehensive IB, dual immersion curriculum equips students with global competencies for success in the real world. As a leader in immersion education, Yu Ying is determined to advance Chinese language programs and global citizenry education by helping other schools create and strengthen their Chinese programs. For more information, email: products@washingtonyuying.org

十二月

星期一	星期二	星期三	星期四	星期五	星期六	星期日
	1	2	3	4	5	6
7	8	9	10	11	12	13
14	15	16	17	18	19	20
21	22	23	24	25	26	27
28	29	30	31			

在十二月,美國有哪些節日呢?有聖誕節,還有光明節和寬扎節。

光明節是猶太人的節日。人們通常會慶祝八天八夜。

慶祝的時候，人們會點蠟燭。每天點一根，一共八根。

這些蠟燭會被放在窗戶旁邊。

在光明節，人們會玩陀螺遊戲。人們還會吃油炸麵團。

十二月

星期一	星期二	星期三	星期四	星期五	星期六	星期日
	1	2	3	4	5	6
7	8	9	10	11	12	13
14	15	16	17	18	19	20
21	22	23	24	25	26	27
28	29	30	31	一月 1		

寬扎節是非洲裔美國人的節日。人們通常會慶祝七天七夜。

慶祝的時候,人們會點蠟燭。每天點一根,一共七根。

家裡的裝飾品，有紅色的，有綠色的，還有黑色的。

人們會唱歌和講故事。

人們還會吃非洲食物。

Glossary

	Pinyin	English Definition
節日	jié rì	festival
聖誕節	shèng dàn jié	Christmas
光明節	guāng míng jié	Hanukkah
寬扎節	kuān zhā jié	Kwanzaa
猶太人	yóu tài rén	Jewish people
慶祝	qìng zhù	to celebrate
蠟燭	là zhú	candle
窗戶	chuāng hù	window
旁邊	páng biān	next to
陀螺	tuó luó	dreidel
油炸麵團	yóu zhá miàn tuán	fried doughnut
非洲裔	fēi zhōu yì	African descent
裝飾品	zhuāng shì pǐn	decoration

www.ingramcontent.com/pod-product-compliance
Lightning Source LLC
Chambersburg PA
CBHW041222070526
44584CB00001B/55